THE ALLIGATOR

MONARCH OF THE MARSH

by Connie Toops

Published by:

**Florida National Parks &
Monuments Association, Inc.**

Homestead, Florida

Acknowledgements

Completion of this book would not have been possible without the support of friends and co-workers at Everglades National Park. I specifically wish to thank Fred and Sandy Dayhoff, Jack de Golia, Dr. Bill Robertson, and Pat Toops for sharing their observations, advice, and encouragement. Thanks go to Dr. Jim Kushlan, Marilyn Kushlan, and their assistants for allowing me to accompany them in the field during the Everglades alligator study. Special thanks also go to Nena Garcia Creasy for her illustrations and enthusiasm throughout the project.

During the revision of this book, the following researchers supplied information on their alligator projects: Mark O. Bara, Robert H. Chabreck, R. Howard Hunt, Ted Joanen, Jim Kushlan, Steve Ruckel, Bruce Thompson, and Kent Vliet. I thank them for their assistance.

Front Cover: A tricolored heron fishes in an Everglades alligator hole. Water birds and other animals stalk warily, keeping their distance from the owner of the hole.

Back Cover: Arching its head and tail, a gator bellows by vibrating air in its throat.

All photos by Connie Toops, unless noted.

Table of Contents

Printed by
Haff-Daugherty Graphics, Inc.
Hialeah, Florida

Designed by Don Platt Advertising

Typography by Supertype, Inc.

Drawings by Nena Garcia Creasy

ISBN 0-945142-00-5

Library of Congress number 79-51891
First printing June 1979
Second printing February 1988

I – The Alligator's Domain

The early stillness of a spring morning is broken by a bass rumble that sounds like thunder. From across the marsh echoes a reply. The trembling rumble is sounded five, perhaps six, times more. Each time the reply rolls back across the water. Then all is silent again. As filmy mists rise from the water's surface, one can almost imagine standing in the midst of a primeval swamp 150 million years ago. In that long-ago era, huge reptiles, some very much like present-day alligators, ruled the tropical marshes. But this is not the world of ages past. The marsh before you may lie in Florida, Georgia, or Louisiana. The coastal plain of the southeastern United States is the alligator's domain.

Climates have cooled and warmed many times in the 150 million years since reptiles ruled the swamps and forests of our planet. Land masses have moved, mountains have risen, and the resulting changes in temperatures and habitats have led to the disappearance of dinosaurs, fish-like lizards, and huge flying reptiles. But in some of the remaining swamps, preserved almost as living fossils, live a few crocodilians. These alligators, crocodiles, and their kin have much the same physical appearance and life style as when they shared the swamps with dinosaurs ages ago.

Crocodilians are scattered around the world in the equatorial belt, but nowhere are they abundant. Thirteen species of crocodiles still exist in isolated spots in the Old and New Worlds. Gharials, slender-snouted fisheaters, inhabit East Indian waters. Five species of caimans live in scattered locations in South and Central America. Only two species of alligators survive – the endangered Chinese and our own American alligator. Populations of almost every one of these crocodilians have dwindled alarmingly in this century as their swampy homes are drained and animals are slaughtered for hides.

What do we know of these living fossils? The American alligator, **Alligator mississippiensis,** and the American crocodile, **Crocodylus acutus,** are the subjects of ongoing studies in this country. Research on crocodilians in other nations is also underway. Scientists have learned a great deal about these reptiles in the past several decades.

Alligators inhabit marshes along the southeastern coastal plain. They hunt, swim, and sun in much the same way as their ancestors have done for millions of years. Photo – C. Walker.

At Home in the Marsh

Before tracing the ancestors of the American alligator, exploring its anatomy, and probing its life history, let us visit the marshland homes of these fascinating reptiles. At Everglades National Park a family walks leisurely along the Anhinga Trail as the children count alligators. They meet a ranger midway through their stroll, and the children excitedly report they have seen thirty-one alligators so far.

"You are lucky," replies the ranger. "If you had visited the park in the summer, you might have seen only one or two. The Everglades has warm, dry winters," he explains. "There is little rain from December through April, and water levels in the marshes drop. Each day of dryness seems to bring another gator or two to the deep ponds like this and the ones at Shark Valley. By the end of the dry season, there may be as many as two hundred alligators at Royal Palm and Shark Valley.

"Once the rainy season begins, usually in May," he continues, "water levels rise. Most of the gators return to the surrounding marshes for the summer and fall. So the best time to see alligators in the Everglades is during the winter and early spring."

A young couple has just returned from paddling a canoe in the Suwannee Canal at Okefenokee National Wildlife Refuge. "We saw several alligators," they tell a ranger at the visitor center, "but all of them were just lying around on the canal bank. Don't they ever **do** anything?"

"Sure they do," answers the ranger, "but the alligators along the canal are accustomed to seeing people float by in canoes. As long as you don't approach too closely, they just lie there quietly. In the backcountry, it's a different story. Where alligators aren't used to seeing people, they slip back into the water and submerge long before you reach them."

"Alligators are cold-blooded," he continues. "Lying in the sun helps regulate the animal's body temperatures. During the spring and fall, and on cool summer mornings, the gators crawl out of the water after sunrise. Their dark skin absorbs heat. Sometimes, especially with the larger alligators, the head heats faster than the massive body. In order to cool their skulls while the rest of the body is still warming, gators open their mouths and pant by moving their throat skin in and out. This circulates cooler air around the head."

"Can they get too hot?" the couple inquires.

"Yes," he replies. "If an alligator becomes too warm, it goes back into the water to cool off. Like humans, alligators are sensitive to too much sun. Many gators lie under willows or other shrubs to avoid being sunburned. They may move into and out of the water several times a day. By dusk, however, the water is usually warmer than the air, and they slide back down the bank. On cool, windy days," he adds, "gators stay in the water, floating with just their eyes and nose exposed."

Visitors at Gulf Islands National Seashore have been patiently watching a large alligator in a bayou. One of the park interpreters joins them. "Why haven't we seen the alligator eat anything?" the visitors ask.

"Since alligators are cold-blooded," she replies, "they don't require as much food as we do. In the summer large alligators may only eat once or twice a week. Gators will eat whenever they can catch prey, but they are most active from dusk to dawn. Come down to the marsh this evening," she suggests. "You'll hear frogs and night herons calling, and you may even be lucky enough to hear the splashing of the gator as it lunges for fish or turtles."

At a lakeside campground in Louisiana, a mother cautions her two sons not to feed the alligator that is lying a few feet offshore. Several minutes later the state park ranger stops at their campsite. "Would that alligator really hurt us?" the boys ask.

"Probably not, but we can't be sure," he replies. "When people feed gators, the animals lose their fear of humans. We suggest that you not approach an alligator closer than about fifteen feet. If it hisses or opens its mouth in defense, you should back away even farther."

"We also advise people not to swim near alligators," he continues. "There have been several incidents in recent years where gators have attacked and drowned swimmers. In a few cases, children playing at the edge of the water have been bitten. These incidents are not common, but still, it pays to be very careful around animals as large and powerful as alligators."

Red-bellied turtle falls victim to an alligator near the Anhinga Trail.

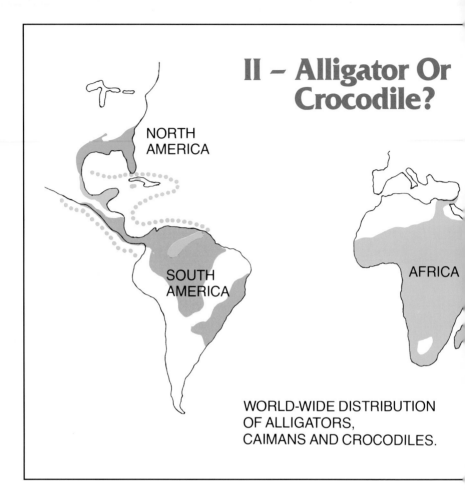

II – Alligator Or Crocodile?

NORTH AMERICA

SOUTH AMERICA

AFRICA

WORLD-WIDE DISTRIBUTION
OF ALLIGATORS,
CAIMANS AND CROCODILES.

Present-day crocodilians may be classified into three separate groups, based on body characteristics and ancestral lines of descent. The largest group, the true crocodiles, is represented by thirteen living species. The second group contains only one species, the slender-snouted gharial. The third group includes alligators and caimans, which are distinctively separate in appearance and ancestors.

True Crocodiles

True crocodiles are found in certain tropical areas throughout the world. They have slender, triangular snouts. The fourth tooth on each side of the lower jaw projects outward slightly and can be seen

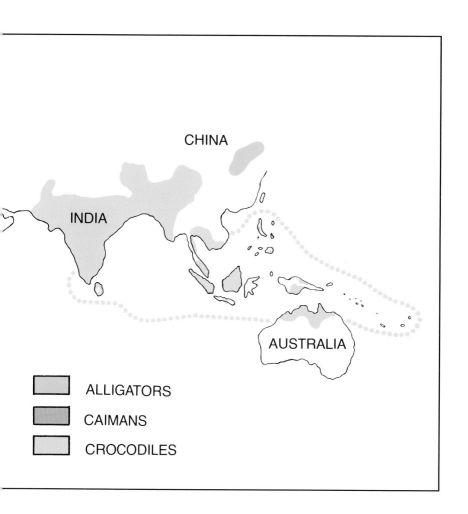

CHINA

INDIA

AUSTRALIA

■ ALLIGATORS

■ CAIMANS

■ CROCODILES

protruding from a notch in the upper jaw. The base color of crocodiles is olive, sometimes with a yellowish or grayish tint. Crocodiles often have bands of black cross markings. Of the thirteen species of crocodiles presently known, four live in the New World, four in Africa, and five in Southeast Asia and Australia.

Some crocodiles inhabit fresh water, while others are found in brackish or salty water. The smallest crocodiles are the four- to five-foot dwarf crocodiles of Africa. The largest known are the seventeen-foot Nile crocodiles and the twenty-foot estuarine crocodiles of the Indonesian islands. Both larger species, as well as the Indian mugger crocodile, have occasionally been known to attack human beings. Most smaller crocodiles are rather timid and retiring.

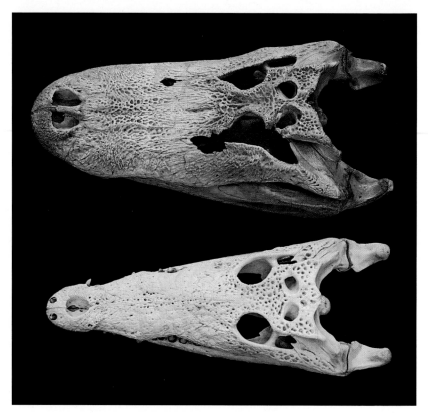

American alligators are more blunt-snouted than American crocodiles, as these skulls show. The alligator is at the top, the crocodile below.

The endangered American crocodile is the only crocodile found in the United States. These shy animals inhabit brackish and coastal waters in the extreme southern Florida. Their last strongholds are Crocodile Lake National Wildlife Refuge at Key Largo and eastern Florida Bay in Everglades National Park. The entire U.S. population includes about 300 to 400 animals. American crocodiles as large as fourteen feet have been recorded, but in the wild it is unusual to see an animal longer than ten feet. American crocodiles also live along the coasts of Central America, northern South America, Cuba, Hispaniola, and Jamaica, but they are quite rare throughout their range.

Gharials

Gharials are recognized by slender snouts lined with 108 needle-like teeth. They live in fresh water streams in eastern India and Nepal and feed exclusively on fish. Hunting and egg-collecting depleted gharial populations to near extinction by 1972. Since then seven wildlife sanctuaries and a program to restock hatchlings have been established.

Gharials grow to a maximum length of twenty feet. Males have a pot-shaped bump on their snouts that seems to amplify their nasal breeding calls. The animals take their name from "ghara," the Hindi word for pot. Gharials are sometimes confused with tomistomas, or "false gharials." Tomistomas also have long snouts and eat fish, but they are members of the true crocodile group. Tomistomas are native to Indonesia.

Alligators and Caimans

The third group of crocodilians includes both alligators and caimans. In general they are stockier and more broad-nosed than crocodiles. Their color is usually darker and their teeth do not protrude as crocodiles' do. Five separate species of caimans are found in scattered fresh-water locations in South and Central America. All of these are dark brown or black, and some have lighter yellowish or orange cross markings. The snout of a caiman is more rounded and wider than most crocodiles' but it is not as blunt as an alligator's. Caimans do not have a bony membrane in the nasal part of the snout as alligators do. They have a greater number of keeled, plate-like bones called "scutes" in the skin behind the head. This gives them a more armored appearance. Most caimans reach a maximum length of six or seven feet, but one species, the black caiman, has been known to grow to lengths of ten to twelve feet. Caimans were sold as pets until the early 1970s. Some that escaped or were set free have survived in the mild climate of southern Florida. A small colony of spectacled caimans lives in the canals east of Homestead, FL.

The only two living species of alligators are found half a world apart. The Chinese alligator is native to the fresh-water marshes of Anhui and Jiangxi, provinces located along the Chang Jiang River in eastern China. This species resembles the American alligator, except that it is shorter and stockier. Animals exceeding five feet are seldom found. The principal food of this alligator may be turtles, although it has only recently begun to be studied. The Chinese alligator was not discovered until 1879 and little has been written about it. It may never have been widespread, and its numbers in the wild now are probably small. A captive-breeding program is underway, with hatchlings being raised at the Bronx and Houston zoos.

The American alligator is native to the southeastern United States. Alligators have blunt, rounded snouts, black upper hides, and their teeth do not project through the skull as crocodiles' do. Teeth are visible, though, when the gators' mouths are shut. Alligators live in freshwater lakes, rivers, and swamps. They occasionally live in brackish water. The name **alligator** is apparently a corruption of "el lagarto," Spanish for lizard.

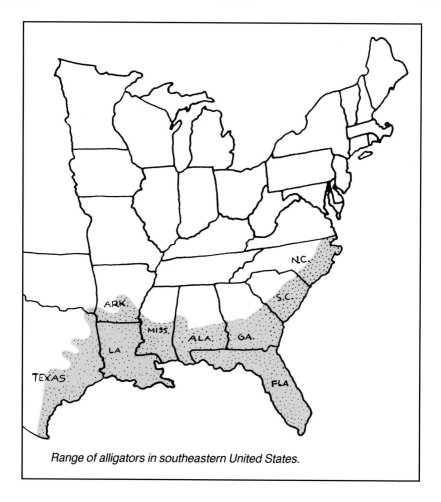

Range of alligators in southeastern United States.

The range of the American alligator extends south from coastal swamps in North and South Carolina to the tip of southern Florida, then west along the Gulf Coast to the mouth of the Rio Grande. Alligators range inland throughout the southern coastal flatlands. They do not inhabit the piedmont and foothills of the Appalachians because the terrain is too hilly and dry and the streams too swift. The coastal plain provides a flatter habitat with more lazily flowing rivers, still water, and swamps. Here temperatures fluctuate less from season to season. The northernmost range of the alligator corresponds roughly to areas of an average January temperature of 45°F (7°C) and an average winter minimum of 15°F (-8°C). Alligators can live successfully in less than tropical temperatures, as long as the cold spells are not too severe or prolonged.

Alligators also range northward along the Mississippi River to about the mouth of the Arkansas River. A few alligators live in rivers in southeastern Oklahoma and occasionally they are reported in northeastern Texas. Increasingly arid conditions determine the western limit of the alligator's range.

Although alligators were once found fairly commonly throughout their range, large populations today are limited to swamps, parks, refuges, and other wetlands where their habitat is protected. Hunting alligators for their hides took an unbelievable toll on their numbers during the last half of the nineteenth century and the first half of the twentieth, but an even greater problem now exists with the destruction of alligator habitat. Many marshes and swamps that formerly supported active alligator populations have been drained in recent years. Farmland, housing developments, highways, and shopping centers now stand where alligators once roamed free. Alligator populations have recovered from illegal hunting. But their numbers will never reach levels they achieved prior to settlement because much of their former wetland habitat is now lost.

The few odd locality records outside the normal range are probably attributable to releases of pets during the years it was legal to sell and possess baby alligators, and not to populations expanding their range. Alligators cannot survive long when released in cold northern climates. Rumors of pet alligators being flushed down toilets and surviving to multiply in the sewer systems of large cities such as New York and Chicago are completely false.

The only place in this country where the ranges of alligators and crocodiles coincide is at the tip of southern Florida. Anywhere else in the Southeast, the crocodilian you may encounter would be an alligator. If you are in southern Florida and there is cause to wonder which animal is being viewed, just remember these identifying characteristics: Alligators have rounded snouts, black hides, and usually live in fresh water. Crocodiles have pointed snouts, greenish-gray hides, and are found in salt water. Since crocodiles are quite rare, the chance of seeing one in the wild is slim.

III – Rumblings From The Past

Why are crocodilians found primarily in tropical and semi-tropical areas? Why are the only two living species of alligators found half a world apart? Why, indeed, are living crocodilians found at all since many of the other animals that evolved at the same time are now extinct?

In order to answer these and other questions about alligators, crocodiles, and related reptiles, scientists must piece together a history of the ages past from fossils and deposits in rock layers formed millions of years ago. As more deposits are analyzed and dated, the store of knowledge of the plants, animals, and climates of the past becomes more complete.

Gaps in the story exist where deposits are scarce. It is difficult for scientists to determine exactly what a living plant or animal looked like from mere fragments of leaves or bones. But from various world-wide discoveries, it is possible to trace fairly accurately the development of alligators and crocodiles.

Ancient Crocodiles

Using the records held in fossils and ancient rock layers, let us return to the earth as it may have appeared some 250 million years ago. Our planet looked very different then. Geologists theorize that a huge continent occupied the area between the equator and the South Pole. It later separated to form the present continents of South America, Africa, Antarctica, and Australia. The huge continent had glaciers to the south and a warmer climate near the equator. A second super-continent lay in the Northern Hemisphere. It later split into the land masses of North America, Europe, and most of Asia. The climate of this giant land mass was fairly warm.

Sea life of this period was diverse, including fishes, amphibians, and a variety of invertebrates (simple animals without backbones). Giant cycads, which were palm-like plants with their seeds in cones, and ferns dotted the landscape. The first reptiles were just beginning to evolve. They were primitive and generalized creatures, ancestors to dinosaurs as well as our modern turtles, lizards, snakes, and crocodilians.

In the 50 million years that followed, the climate was warm and moist. Plant and animal life continued to diversify. Primitive reptiles developed into more specialized forms. Some became huge flesh-and plant-eating dinosaurs and flying reptiles. Others evolved as marine dwelling fish-like lizards, and several groups began to take on forms more like present turtles, snakes, lizards, and mammals. One such group of generalized reptiles, **thecodontia,** is of special interest. It is the group that fostered all later crocodilians.

Thecodonts were small reptiles, four to five feet long, with tails accounting for about half of their length. They had long, slender heads and heavily armored skin. Since fossils show their back legs were longer, they probably walked in an upright position.

Thecodonts were ancestral to many specialized forms of reptiles, including crocodilian descendents. The earliest crocodilian known so far was discovered in fossil beds in western Argentina. Its body shape was similar to present-day crocodiles, although in addition to tooth rows along each jawbone, this creature had teeth in the roof of its mouth. This animal has been named **Proterochampsa,** ancient or forerunning crocodile.

Two similar crocodilians were found in fossil deposits in southern Africa. Remembering that South America and Africa were probably joined as one land mass at that time, it is relatively safe to assume that all were related and evolved from the more generalized thecodonts in the same vicinity at about the same time. The fossil remains of these earliest crocodilians have been found in rock layers believed to be 190 to 200 million years old.

Ages of Change

Years passed, climates remained mild, and marine areas became more widespread. Lower land masses were covered with water. Numerous groups of crocodile-like animals continued to specialize. Some sea dwellers were forty to fifty feet long. Other crocodilians adapted to living in more desert-like conditions in inland areas. Fossil remains reveal dwarfed forms one to three feet long and others with unusually heavy armor. As conditions such as climate and the availability of food and water changed, some were able to adapt to the changes and survived. Many others were too specialized or could not adapt quickly enough and perished. These variously evolving forms, known collectively as the **Mesosuchia,** or intermediate crocodiles, flourished for about 120 million years.

About seventy million years ago our planet underwent another series of changes. Gradually the climate began to cool. At the same time the Rocky Mountains began uplifting, causing the vast sea that covered much of the interior North America to drain. As changes such as these took place around the world, groups of crocodilians became separated from each other. After thousands of years of isolation, they evolved into separate and distinct forms. Take the case of gharials and true crocodiles. About 100 million years ago a common ancestor of both was found on the giant continent in the Southern Hemisphere. Later groups of these animals were divided by the changing terrain. Those living in the waters of India, Africa, and South America specialized in catching fish. They developed the long, slender snouts and sharp teeth characteristic of modern gharials.

Ensuing climatic and habitat changes led to their extinction in South America and presently they are found only in a few freshwater rivers in India and Nepal. About the same time, other separated groups began evolving into different forms, eventually developing into today's American crocodile, Nile crocodile, estuarine crocodile, and so on.

As years passed, our planet began to look more like it does today. Ocean currents changed and there were fewer wetland areas. Temperatures were generally cooler. Plants and animals continued their evolution in response to these changing conditions. Flowering plants replaced many of the more primitive ferns and cycads. Large reptiles such as the dinosaurs gave way to modern forms, including birds and mammals. Many intermediate forms of crocodilians could not keep pace with the changes around them. Generalized animals from the Goniopholidian branch of development – thecodont descendants that had blunt snouts and lived in freshwater areas of Europe and Asia – did survive. It is from these individuals that our modern crocodilians have descended.

Modern Alligators and Crocodiles

Continental shifts and cooling climates caused the warm, moist areas that many crocodilians inhabited to dwindle in size or disappear. Swampy areas became separated by deserts or isolated by large oceans. The ancestors of modern crocodiles were probably first found in Europe, Asia, and North America. Later they spread into Africa and South America. As cooling continued, they gradually disappeared from all but tropical areas.

The first members of the alligator group originated either in Asia or North America from the more generalized "intermediate" crocodilians. Fossils dating to about 70 million years ago confirm that recognizable primitive alligators were present in both Montana and China. The Montana alligator was a medium-sized, rather stocky animal. In the following few million years alligators were also able to inhabit South America and Europe. These primitive South American alligators diversified into the later forms of caimans found there now. The European alligators eventually died out.

As with other crocodilians, alligators diversified throughout the area where they were found. Some were long and heavy; others had thick armor or horns of enlarged head bones. Some were broad-snouted, medium-sized and similar in appearance to modern alligators. Scientists believe one of these forms, **Alligator olseni,** whose remains have been found in Florida deposits that are approximately 20 million years old, was the common ancestor to both living species of alligators today. They believe that our American alligator evolved from **Alligator olseni** about two million years ago.

Researchers believe that **Alligator olseni** gave rise to other forms that moved across the land connection then existing between Alaska and Asia during warmer times about ten million years ago. There it gradually developed and changed, giving rise to the Chinese alligator. At one time both the Chinese and American alligators were much more widespread. As climates cooled during recent ice ages, their ranges became smaller and the two species of alligators became isolated.

Similar species of crocodilians are thus found in widely separated areas today as a result of continental shifting and climatic changes. The alligators and crocodiles that survive today are only a handful compared to the many forms that have evolved and become extinct in the last 150 million years. The forms that survive do so because they and their ancestors were able to adapt to changing conditions around them. This ability to react favorably to change is the key to survival for all species.

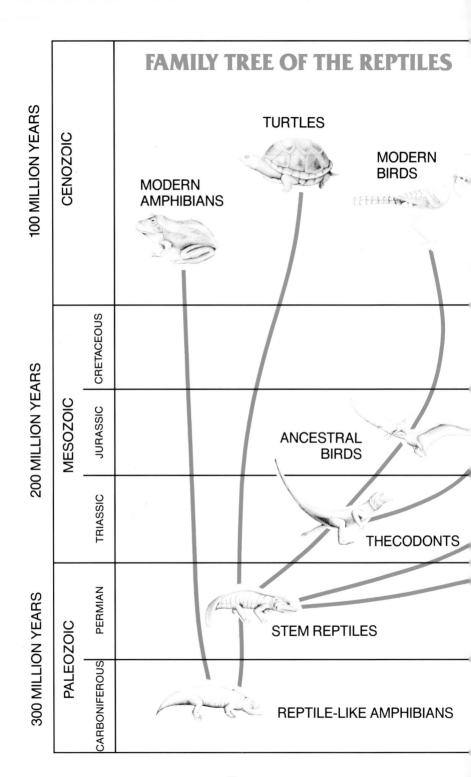

FAMILY TREE OF THE REPTILES

100 MILLION YEARS

CENOZOIC

MODERN AMPHIBIANS

TURTLES

MODERN BIRDS

200 MILLION YEARS

MESOZOIC

CRETACEOUS

JURASSIC

ANCESTRAL BIRDS

TRIASSIC

THECODONTS

300 MILLION YEARS

PALEOZOIC

PERMIAN

STEM REPTILES

CARBONIFEROUS

REPTILE-LIKE AMPHIBIANS

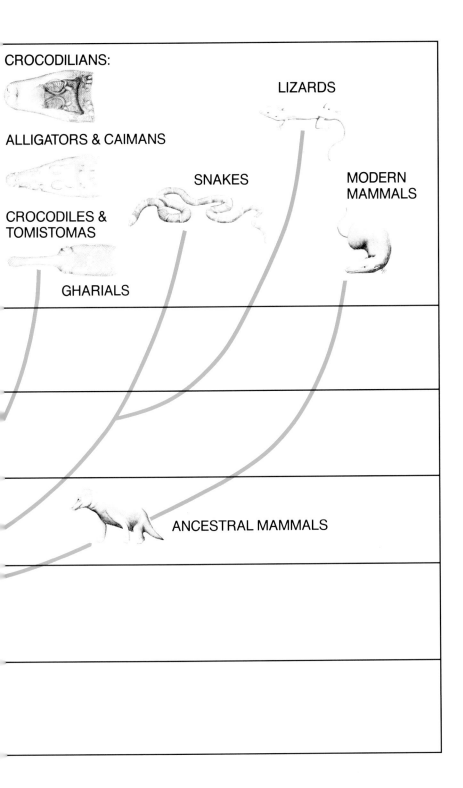

CROCODILIANS:

ALLIGATORS & CAIMANS

CROCODILES &
TOMISTOMAS

GHARIALS

SNAKES

LIZARDS

MODERN
MAMMALS

ANCESTRAL MAMMALS

IV – A Life History

Keen eyes, sharp teeth, and bulging jaw muscles attest to the hunting efficiency of this large gator. Photo – Pat Toops.

Adaptations for Survival

Alligators, crocodiles, and their relatives have survived for millions of years because they have been able to compete favorably for food and living space. As crocodilians evolved, they developed features of anatomy and behavior patterns that allowed them to coexist with birds, mammals, and other advanced forms of life.

Early in their evolution, ancestral reptiles developed methods of internal fertilization and hard-shelled eggs. They could thus reproduce on dry land rather than depositing jelly-like eggs in the water. These were great advances over more primitive reptiles and amphibians. They insured greater success in reproduction. Crocodilians also acquired sharp teeth, claws, and tough, scaly skin that added both to their protection and their efficiency as predators.

Crocodilians evolved with specialized organs, such as well developed middle ear bones and a diaphragm in the chest cavity, that other modern reptiles do not possess. As the muscles of the diaphragm contract and relax, they push the liver forward and back in a pumping action. Air rushes into the lungs as the liver is pulled rearward. It is forced out as the liver moves forward again.

Crocodilians possess a four-chambered heart for more efficient blood circulation. Amphibians and most other reptiles have two-chambered hearts. The more complex circulatory system is beneficial when alligators stay underwater for long periods. Alligators hold their breath underwater. When submerged, blood is routed through the heart to bypass the lungs. Since the lungs cannot contribute fresh supplies of oxygen while underwater, bypassing them conserves oxygen for the remaining organs. The amount of time gators can remain submerged depends upon their size and the temperature of the water. On warm days, they can stay underwater at least 45 minutes. In cooler weather when alligators' metabolic rates are slower, they can remain submerged much longer.

Crocodilians have socketed teeth that grow from holes in the jaw bone. The teeth are hollow and conical. New teeth begin forming under the old caps, replacing old broken ones. Although their brain is not large in comparison to birds or mammals, crocodilian brains do possess a small cerebral cortex, the portion of the brain that controls conscious thought. Most of the crocodilian's specializations add to its efficiency as a predator and increase its chances for survival. Even though crocodilians are more advanced than other reptiles in some features of anatomy, they still depend upon quick, strong muscles to catch prey and tough hides for defense. As the chart below shows, skin and muscle account for most of an alligator's body weight.

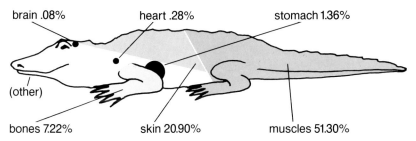

brain .08% heart .28% stomach 1.36%

(other)

bones 7.22% skin 20.90% muscles 51.30%

Average proportion of body weight made up by various organs of an American alligator.

Crocodilians are cold-blooded, which means that their body temperatures fluctuate in response to the temperature of their surroundings. This may be an advantage, because crocodilians live in areas that are warm most of the time. They expend little energy maintaining high body temperatures, so most of their food becomes energy used for growth, tissue maintenance and movement. Having a fairly slow metabolism, crocodilians can survive on much less food and survive times of food scarcity much better than mammals. In one series of experiments, healthy alligators went six months without food. Although they were emaciated, they were still active and recovered quickly when fed. In comparison, mammals require huge amounts of food energy for growth, movement, and temperature regulation. For instance, under similar temperature conditions, in a given length of time, a human would consume ten to twenty times as much oxygen, an indicator of metabolic rates, as an alligator. Since they need less food and have been able to compete successfully with mammals for habitat, crocodilians have been able to survive for such a long time.

The Armored Lizard

American alligators are elongated animals with blunt snouts, four short legs, and a long muscular tail. They swim well, using primarily a side-to-side motion of the tail for propulsion. On land they walk slowly and clumsily, dragging their tails and often flopping down to rest after a few steps. They can move more rapidly on land if they wish, using a "high walk" in which the body is held higher off the ground. They have webbed feet with five toes on each front foot and four toes on each back foot. The fourth and fifth (outer) toes on each front foot and the fourth (outer) toe on the back foot are clawless. Each of the other toes ends in a sharp claw. Alligators can move around well on land or in the water, although they are most often seen at rest. Young alligators are especially agile. They climb well, often clambering over each other, rocks, and branches.

An alligator's skull is quite heavy and the jaws are hinged well back, allowing the mouth to open wide. Mature alligators have about forty teeth each in the upper and lower jaw. All of the teeth are not usually present, however, because they occasionally break off after biting hard objects. Teeth are replaced regularly when the alligator is young, but in older animals broken teeth may not be replaced. While all teeth are the same shape, some are larger than others. All alligators have sharp teeth; there are no molars for crushing and grinding food.

On land alligators usually walk slowly, dragging their tails and stopping to rest after a few steps. They can move faster over shorter distances using a "high walk" in which the body is carried farther off the ground.

Alligators have tremendous power in closing their jaws, but the muscles to reopen them are much weaker. It is true that most alligators' mouths can be held shut by gripping and holding both jaws together. But once a large alligator's jaws have clamped down, it is almost impossible for anyone to pry them open. Folk tales maintain that alligators' jaws are hinged from the top and crocodiles' from the bottom, but this is merely legend. Alligators and crocodiles open their mouths in exactly the same manner, the same way human beings do.

The inner mouth lining of an alligator is a soft, skin-like pink tissue. Alligators have tongues, but the tongue is attached along the "floor" of the mouth and does not protrude. A fold of this tissue at the back of the mouth covers the throat opening to close it off when the alligator submerges. Alligators do have sensory cells, probably for taste and perhaps smell, in the lip scales along the upper and lower jaws.

The hide of an alligator is very tough, formed of hundreds of rectangular scales. Scales on the neck, back, upper tail, and sides have bony plates, called scutes, embedded in them. This gives alligators an armored appearance. Scales under the throat, on the belly, and under the tail have no scutes. When alligators are hunted for their hides, only this unarmored, creamy white undersection is skinned out and made into wallets, shoes, and handbags. The upper body of an alligator is black. Juveniles have yellowish cross-hatching that helps camouflage them amid marsh grasses.

An alligator's head is elongated and flattened, ending in a rounded snout. The head is attached to the body by a short, thick neck. Two nasal openings located at the tip of the snout have crescent-shaped flaps of skin that close over them when the alligator swims underwater. Farther back on the head lie a pair of outward-looking eyes. Alligator eyes are similar in appearance to human eyes. They have a wide field of vision, and gators seem to see well even at night. The pupils of the eyes are green in young alligators, turning brown in older individuals. They have a vertical slit similar to a cat's eye for light to pass through. Viewed at night with a flashlight, the eyes of all alligator reflect ruby red. Alligators have two sets of eyelids. One set is much like ours, closing from top to bottom. The second set is transparent and closes from front to rear. This enables the alligator to see while swimming underwater but still have sensitive eye tissue protected.

The ears of an alligator are not prominent as they are in mammals. They are located immediately behind the eyes and have a covering flap of skin to keep water out. Alligators seem to hear quite well, perhaps even distinguish between the voices of others of their kind. Alligators often rest or hunt while partially submerged. Usually only the head is above water. With their body in this position, sensory lip scales lie just at the water line, and the eye, nose, and ears are exposed. This enables the alligator to breathe, see, hear, and probably taste and smell, while only a small portion of its body is out of the water and visible to predators or potential victims. From this position gators can inch forward toward prey or submerge quickly and quietly, leaving hardly a ripple on the water's surface.

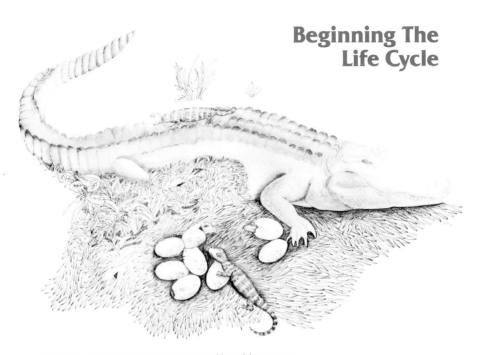

Beginning The Life Cycle

Female alligator guards her nest of hatching young.

Early in September baby alligators emerge from their leathery eggs. All eggs hatch about the same time, and the babies begin to give grunting calls. If the mother is nearby, she will dig into the nest of cattails or marsh grasses. Gently she will grasp the wiggling babies in her mouth and carry them from the nest to open water. If the mother is not present, some of the babies will squirm free and instinctively head for the water. Hatchlings buried deep in the nest may not be able to free themselves, and they will perish.

Baby alligators measure eight or nine inches in length when they hatch. They feed on their own, but usually remain in the group with their mother. In her presence, they have a much better chance of survival. The babies' grunts help the female keep track of the brood. When young gators are threatened, they utter a distress call that brings the mother hissing and lunging at predators. In one study, a young gator was caught and held until the mother burst from the water to recover it. After the baby was released, the mother gingerly picked it up in her mouth and carried it back to the water.

Young alligators fend for themselves. They have quick reflexes and sharp teeth. Young gators lie in shallow water snapping at flies, water beetles, and other insects. They also catch small fish, crayfish, snails, and tadpoles. How quickly they grow depends upon air temperatures and the abundance of food.

A baby alligator, approximately six months old, suns on an alligator flag leaf.
Photo – Pat Toops.

In southern Florida alligators hatch when water levels are high and food is scattered. Although they remain active through the winter, they seldom grow much. In northern parts of their range, young alligators feed for a few weeks in the fall. With the onset of winter, they enter a period of dormancy. Many of the small gators lose weight and shrink slightly in length during this period. As temperatures warm again in the spring and summer, food becomes more available and they grow much faster.

After their first winter, young alligators grow slightly less than one foot per year for the next four to five years. Some mother gators have two broods with them at once. The ten-inch hatchlings are easy to distinguish from the yearlings, which are about twice that size. It is during this period that young gators are most vulnerable to predators. A large percentage of the hatchlings die within their first two years. Great blue herons, great egrets, large bass, otters, and raccoons all eat small alligators. The large wading birds have been observed stalking near dens day after day, waiting for the chance to pick off another baby.

Young alligators usually stay near the nest or den area. They feed, grunt to each other, and sun on rocks, branches, or mother's back. During the dry season they may move to a deeper hole in search of standing water. Drought periods are especially hard on first- and second-year animals. Alligators less than four years old usually do not make holes or dens of their own. During these times of dryness, they concentrate around the few remaining water holes, where they are more vulnerable to predation by birds, mammals, and sometimes other alligators. It is true that alligators will eat their own kind, but generally this happens only during times of stress, such as severe dry spells.

Reaching Adulthood

After young alligators leave their mothers, they tend to roam. They also have good homing instincts. Several Louisiana gators returned home from experimental releases as far as twelve miles away. Adult alligators have covered even more remarkable distances. An older alligator was removed from Nine Mile Pond in Everglades National Park because it had been fed by too many visitors and was becoming too bold. It was released at Shark Valley, but in two months appeared at Nine Mile Pond again, traveling a distance of 35 miles. Scientists at a Louisiana refuge traced by radio telemetry the path of an energetic adult gator that moved 5.2 miles in one day.

Rangers removing the one-eyed gator from Nine Mile Pond in Everglades National Park. It returned, covering a straight-line distance of 35 miles in about two months. NPS Photo.

Scientists are not certain what triggers an alligator's urge to roam. The stimulus may be fluctuations in water levels or territorial instincts brought on by hormonal changes. For females this urge decreases by the time they reach five to ten years of age. At maturity, females establish a nesting territory and afterward seldom range more than one-half mile from this den. Males usually wander more, especially during and after the breeding season. Their home range may be large as 2000 acres.

As alligators mature, their vocalizations change. Instead of grunting, adult alligators communicate using bellows, head slaps and hisses. Alligators hiss by passing air through their throats. They hiss loudly when upset, especially when approached too closely by humans. Head slaps are popping noises made when gators lie with their head and tail out of the water, then quickly open their mouths and slap the lower jaw on the water's surface. This noise, resulting from the snapping jaws hitting the water, is often heard as mating season approaches. It may trigger answering slaps from nearby gators. Both males and females have the ability to bellow. Bellows

Arching its head and tail, a gator bellows by vibrating air in its throat.

sound like the rumbling of thunder or a jet aircraft and can be heard as far as one-half mile on still days. Individual alligators have distinctive voices, perhaps recognizable to other alligators. The rhythm of the male's series of bellows is noticeably slower than the female's. Most bellowing seems to take place early on warm spring mornings, but alligators have been known to bellow at any time and any season.

Bellowing may take place either on land or in the water. In the water, the gator arches its head and tail and lets its belly sink below the surface. In a rocking motion the gator takes in some air, sinks slightly, and vibrates its throat. Contrary to what might be expected, the mouth is not opened. Male alligators' throats often vibrate enough to set the water around them in motion. The motion is similar to the splashing that occurs when a vibrating tuning fork is lowered into a pan of water. A few folk stories insist that alligators spray musk when they bellow, but in reality it is the vibrating water, not musk that is seen as the animals sound off.

Alligators have musk glands, one on either side of the throat and one at the cloaca (the outer opening of the intestinal, urinary, and genital tracts). When alligators bellow, the tiny throat glands are turned inside out. It is possible that some musky substance is dispensed, but the smell is not apparent near bellowing gators. Sometimes when larger alligators are handled, the musky odor can be detected. The functions of musk and musk glands are not yet completely understood.

Bellowing is most common in the spring, peaking during the courtship period in May. Bellowing may be more than a method for male and female alligators to notify each other of their presence. Some scientists have suggested it also helps disperse alligators more evenly throughout a particular habitat. By bellowing and giving head-slaps, dominant males hope to attract several female mates into their territories. Juvenile males may be warned by this behavior to remain outside the social circles of the large bulls.

Alligators also communicate by watching each other. Usually male and female alligators have a well established "peck order" hierarchy in which larger and more powerful alligators, simply by their presence, induce smaller gators to give up sunning posts on the bank or resting places in shallow water. Usually there is no physical contact between individuals. Larger gators cruise slowly through the water, coming to rest near the spot they desire. If a smaller gator is occupying that position, it carefully watches the movements of the larger competitor. When the larger gator begins to come out of the water, the smaller one usually leaves its position. Sometimes it just moves a few feet to one side or the other. During courtship alligators of opposite sexes are not so quick to move away from each other.

The breeding season corresponds to warming temperatures and lengthening days of spring and early summer. Although some courtship activities begin as early as mid-February in southern Florida, the main part of the breeding season extends from mid-April through May. Breeding and nesting activities are somewhat affected by water levels and temperatures, so exact dates vary from year to year.

During the mating season, alligators allow close approach by members of the opposite sex. Some even tolerate mates resting with their heads or forelimbs on their backs. NPS Photo by M.W. Williams.

As courtship activities progress, one alligator will allow close and peaceful approach by another alligator of the opposite sex. Although bellowing may play a role in bringing gators together, the courtship proceeds quietly. Courting pairs may swim in the same vicinity for several days before mating occurs. They may also sun together. Sometimes the female even permits the male to stroke her back with his forelimb. Courtship continues in the water, where both individuals approach each other quietly.

Usually the smaller female gator swims to the male. They float with their heads together, bodies angling away. The female may swim around the male, sometimes touching noses or necks. The male may submerge and blow a stream of bubbles past the female's head. Behaviorists have watched courting gators test one another's strength by trying to gently press each other under water. Eventually the female swims alongside the male. She bends her tail slightly upward and both submerge. Copulation takes place underwater, usually lasting about thirty seconds. The two alligators may, but do not necessarily, remain in the same vicinity for a short while after mating. Male alligators probably mate with several females during the same season.

A Nest of Cattails and Sawgrass

Female alligators normally begin to nest two months after the onset of courtship. This may be speeded up or slowed several weeks by local temperature conditions. In southern Florida, nesting activities begin in mid-June, normally after the annual rainy season has begun. In northern areas, nesting peaks in late June. By this time males have abandoned their mates. Nest building and guarding are the exclusive duty of the female.

A mound of sawgrass and cattails protects alligator eggs as they incubate.

Nest sites may be on slightly higher banks or on the edge of small bay heads. They are often shaded by willows and cattails. Nests may be ten to fifteen feet from the water or located in the open marsh. Females sometimes nest in the same vicinity from year to year but the actual nest site is seldom reused.

The nest mounds are usually high enough to keep the eggs from being flooded by subtle fluctuations in water levels. Researchers in southern Florida have found that untimely large releases of water from management areas result in widespread nest flooding and drowning of the developing eggs.

Once the nest is constructed, the female digs a cavity in the top of the nest with her hind feet. She will lay about one egg every 30 to 45 seconds, finishing the task in approximately an hour. The egg cavity measures about nine inches in diameter and seven inches deep. As the female lays the leathery eggs, she pushes them into the cavity with her hind foot. Once she finishes, the female gator pushes more vegetation over the top of the nest and packs it gently with her foot.

Young females generally nest every other year and lay fewer eggs than fully mature ones. Very old alligators do not nest at all. Everglades alligator nests usually contain about 30 eggs. In northern areas, 38 to 39 eggs are more typical. There is great variation from nest to nest. Some hold as few as 20; others, 50 or more. One Louisiana nest was filled with 88 eggs. The incubation period for alligator eggs is 65 to 70 days, depending upon air temperatures. Typically, nests completed by late June hatch in early September.

The urge for females to guard their nests may be stronger at the beginning of the incubation period. Some stray during midsummer but return about the time the eggs hatch. Others remain near the nest site for the duration. They hiss and lunge at human intruders. They capture and eat marauding raccoons or fight with bears and wild boars trying to raid the eggs. When females are diligent in guarding their nests, the young have a much greater chance of hatching.

Alligator eggs are oval, measuring about three inches long and one and three-quarters inches wide. The eggs are the same size at both ends, and the shell is two-layered. The outer part is hard and thicker than the shell of a chicken's egg. The inner layer is a thick

Young gators such as these are usually under the watchful eye of their mother, buy many fall prey to predators. Photo – C. Walker.

membrane. At about the seventh week, the shell begins to develop a network of tiny cracks all over the outside. It is thought that bacteria from the moist nest cavity aid in the deterioration of the tough shells.

Inside the egg a light yellow yolk and stiff albumen nourish the development of the baby alligator. The tiny gator's head is curled inward around the belly. The abdomen is swollen by the protruding yolk sac. Just before hatching a small "egg tooth" develops at the end of the snout. When the incubation period is up, the little gator tears through the outer membranes of the shell and wiggles out into the nest cavity. As they excavate a nest cavity, female alligators will cautiously bite down on unhatched eggs. If babies are not yet free of the shell, the mother will carry them to the water in her mouth and rinse them off. Mothers frequently swallow eggs that have failed to hatch.

Female alligators do not incubate their nests by sitting on them as birds do. Instead the construction of the nest helps to maintain a fairly constant incubation temperature. The damp, decaying plant material insulates the eggs from quick changes in outside temperatures and humidity. Generally, temperatures inside the test are slightly cooler than outside during the day and slightly warmer at night. Humidity inside the nest reaches 90% or above. Interestingly, the sex of the babies is determined by the temperature inside the nest during the first three weeks of incubation. Eggs at temperatures greater than 91 °F (34 °C) all develop into males. Eggs at less than 85 °F (30 °C) all develop into females. In the wild, nests are frequently warmer at the top than on the sides and bottom. Thus males develop in upper layer and females from lower positions.

An unfortunate turtle becomes lunch for a large alligator.

Lunch With A Gator

An alligator might appear to be sleeping or floating obliviously when it will suddenly lunge for a bird or fish that approaches too closely. This is an opportunistic method of feeding, but sometimes it works. Alligators also grab fish or turtles while submerged. They avoid swallowing large quantities of water by keeping their throat flaps closed.

A gator actively searching for prey often singles out a victim and stalks it. It may try to corner the animal. A hunting alligator moves slowly and deliberately, floating with eyes and nose exposed. Sometimes the gator will submerge when it is ten feet or so from the prey. It lunges after moving closer underwater. At other times it will stop near shore, then jump out of the water. Alligators try to catch their victims with the side of the jaw rather than head on, for a better grip. They seldom stalk prey while on land, probably because they move more slowly and clumsily.

Some alligators appear excited while hunting. Their tails twitch, similar to a hunting cat. After lunging for something and missing, they seem upset. They turn away abruptly, sometimes making quick, usually unsuccessful, lunges at other groups of birds or other alligators. Some appear to sulk, swimming to shore, and with their heads close to land, jerking their tails rapidly back and forth as if angered.

Since alligators are cold-blooded, how frequently they eat depends upon their surroundings. Gators are most likely to feed between dusk and dawn when it is calm and temperatures are above 73°F (23°C). If it is colder, they seldom eat. In laboratory studies, alligators grow best at 81°F (28°C). Smaller alligators have higher metabolic rates. They eat more often, but consume less volume at a time, than large ones.

Alligators do not eat their food in small bits as a human would do. All of their teeth are sharp for cutting and holding rather than blunt, like molars, for crushing. If an item of prey is small in relation to the size of the alligator, it may be swallowed whole. Otherwise the gator will bite down on it repeatedly. Using a combination of sharp teeth and tremendously strong jaw muscles, it breaks bones or shells so the whole item can be swallowed. In the case of large turtles or wading birds, this process may take several hours. Large items may also be shaken vigorously and slapped against the water or shore to rip off swallowing-sized pieces. Alligators will eat carrion.

Big gators have been observed eating deer or other alligators. Alligators roll underwater with large prey, submerging the victim and drowning it. The dead prey is dragged around or guarded for several days until the meat rots enough to be ripped apart. Alligators eat a wide variety of foods including fish, turtles, snakes, frogs, crabs, coots, grebes, wading birds, raccoons, and otters. The splashing of one alligator feeding is a stimulus for surrounding gators to investigate. They may attempt to steal the prey, provoking rolling fights and splashing chases. After one gator has finished feeding, others will sometimes swim to the site and roll their heads back and forth over the feeding area, perhaps in search of scraps.

Watching an alligator dine on a turtle or another alligator is an awesome experience. The tough shell of a foot-long turtle can be crushed in a single bite. Biologists have measured the closing power of alligator jaw muscles at over 3000 pounds per square inch.

Although alligators are carnivorous, they are occasionally seen uprooting cattails and other aquatic vegetation. Evidently they do not eat the plant material, but they may be catching small forms of aquatic animal life such as crayfish, snails, and insects living in the mud at the bases of the plants.

An alligator's digestive system is fairly simple, consisting of a two-parted stomach, an intestine, and a cloacha. After food is swallowed, the gizzard-like first section of the stomach crushes any remaining large pieces. Alligators occasionally eat hard, non-food materials. Food sampling and dissections of several gizzards have revealed an assortment of hard objects including pebbles, stones, hard pieces of wood, and even pop bottles. These are probably used in the gizzard to aid in the crushing process. The stomach of an alligator found dead on a coastal barrier island contained remains of a loon, blue crab shells, pine cones, and about a pound of sand. The sand was probably a substitute for gizzard stones since no rocks existed on the island.

The second lobe of a gator's stomach secretes strong digestive juices. Once pulverized, food from the gizzard enters this lobe and is more thoroughly dissolved and digested. Usually it takes food two days to leave both lobes of an alligator's stomach. By then it is so completely digested there is little trace of hair, bones, shells, or scales in the excrement. Alligators in captivity in a warm environment process a normal meal from eating to excrement in three to five days. "Normal" meals consist of about twenty percent of the alligator's weight. Larger meals take as long as a week to digest.

How Old? How Big?

Among the largest alligators recorded recently were the 17 foot 5 inch gator killed at Apopka, FL, in 1956 and the 17 footer killed in 1973 on Sanibel Island, FL. Historically, the record belongs to a Louisiana gator killed in 1890. It measured 19 feet, 2 inches. Alligators over 14 feet are seldom seen today.

Under ideal conditions, alligators need 72 to 76 months of active growth to reach a length of 6 feet. Since ideal conditions do not occur throughout the alligator's range, growth rates are variable. In southern Florida, temperatures are warm enough for alligators to be active most of the year. But Everglades marshes do not support the densities of fishes, turtles, frogs, and other foods that the peat marshes of Louisiana do. Even though Louisiana gators are active fewer months (usually April through October), they grow slightly faster because of the abundance of food. In North Carolina, the coolest part of the alligator's range, active growth occurs only from May through September. These alligators may take up to twice as long to reach the same length as Louisiana gators.

Male and female alligators grow at similar rates until about 3 feet. Then females grow more slowly. A Louisiana study revealed males at age 10 averaged 8.4 feet, while 10-year-old females were only 6.9 feet long. Females reached 8.4 feet by age 20. Males achieved 11.5 feet by that age. The study predicted female gators living to be 45 years old could reach 9 feet. If males lived to be 80, they could measure 14 feet long.

When alligators are submerged, it is difficult to estimate their length. If the head is visible, the distance in **inches** from the tip of the nose to the eye approximates the distance in **feet** from the tip of the nose to the tail. It is safe to assume any alligator over nine feet is male. Otherwise there is no way to differentiate between the sexes from a distance.

Male alligators may live longer than females. In the wild it is doubtful that males regularly reach more than thirty to thirty-five years of age before the first signs of senility appear. Senility in alligators includes a loss of vigor and appetite, cessation of reproduction, occasional skin lesions, and loss of teeth. In captivity, where they are fed and experience less competition, several have been kept about fifty years. Female alligators have attained an age of thirty years or so in captivity, but probably few live that long under natural conditions. Certainly neither sex reaches the ages of 200 to 250 years claimed by some tourist attractions.

V – Where Do They Live?

A typical scene at an Everglades alligator hole. Photo – C. Walker.

The Gator Hole

In normal years South Florida receives heavy rains during the summer and fall months and experiences a winter and spring dry season. The Everglades environment is thus much wetter from June through November than any other time of the year. During times of high water, alligators range freely throughout the fresh-water sawgrass marshes. During the dry season they seek out, or in some cases engineer, deeper holes that hold water while surrounding areas are drying.

These holes are often associated with clumps of cypress or willow trees, where soil is soft and mucky. In these areas the limestone bedrock eroded thousands of years ago to form pits and holes several feet below the surrounding marsh floor. Over the years these eroded pockets have filled with deep, muddy soil. Alligators wallow out the mud and sediment by swimming and by pushing out mud with their heads and flanks. Once excavated, these holes are used year after year.

Alligator holes are usually ten feet or more in diameter, with the deeper portion, three or four feet deep, located somewhere in the center. Slightly raised banks of mud surround the hole. These mud banks support a lush growth of pond plants in addition to the cypress or willow. Other trees and shrubs commonly associated with gator holes include pond apple, sweet bay magnolia, red bay and cocoplum. The smaller green plants include pickerelweed, arrow-root, swamp lily, marsh and swamp ferns, sawgrass, cattail, several

During the dry season, alligators push mud to the sides of their holes, deepening them as water levels drop.

types of algae, and various aquatic pondweeds. Many of these plants are trampled down along the edge of the water where gators have favorite sunning spots and along trails leading from the hole out into the marsh.

Many alligator holes have caves or dens associated with them. Usually these are dug back into the bank or under the root systems of the willow thickets. Some of the dens extend ten feet or more horizontally under the surface. During times of extreme dryness, a gator may crawl back into the den to escape the hot sun. Sometimes, if the water in their hole dries up, gators will simply wait out the dry season in their dens rather than moving to a new location closer to food and water. Not all gators have dens. Some range throughout freshwater marshes without having a particular hole or den. Others live along the tributary creeks and mangrove-lined headwaters between fresh and saline waters. These animals may move up or down the creek depending upon the salt concentrations in the water, which vary with the season.

Tri-colored herons are among the wading birds that use gator ponds during the dry season. These long-legged hunters stalk warily, keeping their distance from the owner of the hole.

Historically alligator holes in the Everglades retained water throughout the dry season. Recently this has not always been the case. Man-made canals and water diversion projects have altered the amounts of water available to the park. In many years this has the effect of making the dry season longer and more severe, and alligator holes have gone dry. A new management plan calls for releasing water into the park based on seasonal rainfall. It is hoped that this will return more natural water patterns, and better conditions for alligator reproduction, to southern Florida.

A Dry Season Refuge

Freshwater shrimp (prawns), gar, and snails live with alligators in their water holes year-round. So do smaller fish, including topminnows, flagfish, killifish, and sailfin mollies. Water snakes, frogs, anhingas, green-backed herons and common moorhens inhabit the surrounding willow or cypress thickets. As water levels in the marsh begin to drop in the spring, the gator hole becomes more crowded with seasonal tenants.

Marsh-dwelling fishes such as the sunfish, bass, bullhead, bowfin, and shiner gradually migrate toward the deeper water. Turtles, too, begin to seek out gator holes. A few mud, musk, red-bellied, snapping, and softshell turtles live in these holes most of the year, but in the dry season many more congregate there. Long-legged great blue herons are among the first birds to drop in to feast on the increasing fish populations. They are solitary feeders, stalking quietly through belly-deep water at the edge of the hole.

As the dry-down continues, great egrets, little blue herons, white ibis, wood storks, and snowy egrets arrive. Occasionally roseate spoonbills may even find their way to some of the holes. They wade and probe for the small fish, snails, and crayfish in the shallow water. The presence of a few birds seems to encourage more to join the flock. Most of the birds arrive at dawn and feed busily for several hours. Some may fly off during the middle of the day or roost in the trees surrounding the hole. Before dusk there is often another feeding session.

As the dry season progresses, raccoons, otters, and bobcats visit the hole more often. With the abundance of life congregated at the gator hole, finding food becomes an easy task for these predators. In some years oxygen levels in the ponds drop so low that many of the fish die. Then grackles, red-winged blackbirds, and vultures move in to feast on the carrion.

Once the water table begins to drop, tiny fish are caught and concentrated in the gator holes, attracting herons, ibis, egrets, spoonbills, and numerous other wading birds.

Undoubtedly a few of the fish, turtles, birds, and other visitors to the gator hole are eaten by the proprietor. The rest, however, are able to survive the times of dryness as a direct result of the refuge they find in gator holes. Studies have actually shown that when surpluses of fish are eaten by the alligator and visiting wading birds, the few that remain are better able to stand the stresses of the low oxygen levels in the water than if none had been eaten. Thus the alligator and the alligator hole are tremendously important factors in the complex ecological picture of the Florida Everglades.

During the summer and fall when water levels are high and alligators are dispersed widely throughout the marshes, they do not seem especially protective of territories. Sometimes several alligators of various sizes will share the same hole or marsh area. As drying conditions set in, however, alligators do occasionally fight with each other. It seems that larger alligators may choose not to share their holes with other adult or sub-adult gators. Fights sometimes result from this territorial behavior, and occasionally combatants lose limbs, part of their tails, or even their lives in their struggle to occupy a certain area. At this time information on alligator behavior is too incomplete to determine why some adult and sub-adult alligators will peacefully share a water hole while others fight to their deaths to drive competitors out.

A victim of territorial struggle with another alligator, this creature lost its tail, but escaped with its life.

Within the Everglades area, some of the higher pineland ridges have deeply eroded solution holes and caves in the limestone "pinnacle" rock. At one time, prior to drainage and the general lowering of the water table, these holes were partially filled with water during the dry season and were often occupied by alligators. Reports indicate that it was not uncommon to see alligators throughout the pinelands. In recent years few alligators have been seen in these holes. Those that do set up residence in the pinelands solution holes sometimes become trapped at the bottom of the rocky, steep-sided holes as water levels drop in the spring.

Mute testimony to the "survival of the fittest," one gator prepares to eat an invader of its territory.

*An aerial view of Rookery Branch, a part of Shark Slough. This area is represent-
ative of alligator habitat within Everglades National Park and Big Cypress National Preserve.*

Swamps and Bayous

The gator hole serves its main purpose in areas of seasonal water
level fluctuation. In the northern parts of the alligator's range, gator
holes are not as common. Instead, gators excavate dens in river
banks and at the edges of shallow ponds. Here they sluggishly pass
the cool winter months. Gators may sun at the mouth of the den on
warm winter days, but they seldom venture out to hunt.

Alligator habitat in northern areas consists of brackish coastal
marshes, freshwater marshes, wooded swamps, and meandering
rivers. Gator populations are concentrated near the coasts.
Cordgrass, wiregrass, cattails, and rushes provide cover and nesting materials in these marshes. Cypress and gum trees, myrtle and
buttonbush shrubs, and broadleaved aquatic plants vegetate the
swamps and river banks.

Man-Made Habitats

The Southeast has experienced a tremendous increase in its human population over the past century. In the process of building new homes and shopping areas, a number of wetlands have been drained or destroyed. Alligators that formerly lived in these wetlands have moved into farm ponds, borrow pits, quarries, canals, golf course ponds, and lakes in housing developments. Although these bodies of water give alligators a home, they may be so steep-sided or lacking in plant cover that the animals cannot nest. They also do not support the diversity of fishes, turtles, wading birds, raccoons, otters, and bobcats found in undisturbed wetlands.

When alligators live close to residential areas, problems arise. In the wild, alligators tend to avoid humans, and humans usually avoid alligators. An alligator in the pond behind a condominium, however, may become the neighborhood "pet." Well-meaning residents toss it chicken scraps and other tidbits of food. Before long, the gator becomes accustomed to the handouts and loses its inhibitions. As a result, it may lunge at the family dog or children teasing it. The "pet" has suddenly become a nuisance, and in many cases conservation officers are called to move or shoot the alligator.

On a more positive note, many of the marshes that have been diked for mosquito control, oil exploration, or water management uses are still suitable for alligators. Several of the wildlife refuges on the Texas and Louisiana coasts are mazes of dikes and impoundments, and alligator populations are flourishing there. Studies indicate that males and older juveniles inhabit the deeper canals. Females prefer shallower interior marshes.

Where protected from poaching and provided with suitable habitat, alligators are holding their own. The key to the survival of these fascinating relics from the Age of Reptiles is preservation of enough wetland that they may roam and reproduce undisturbed.

VI – A History Of Hunting

Alligators must have existed in amazing abundance in the southeastern coastal plains prior to exploration and settlement by Europeans. Diaries of early settlers describe scenes of river banks lined with alligators and ponds so full of the creatures that one adventurous enough could walk across the pond stepping from back to back. The size and numbers of alligators may have been exaggerated somewhat in these enthusiastic accounts of the first travelers in a new land, but it is certain that alligators did exist in greater numbers than we might imagine today.

Hide Hunting Becomes Profitable

Many of the first settlers considered alligators a nuisance and killed them to protect livestock or merely for sport. Then in 1855 another reason to kill alligators surfaced – their hides. Tanners and manufacturers of leather goods in France discovered that alligator and other crocodilian hides could be made into durable, beautiful products including shoes and saddlebags. The sport of alligator hunting turned into a profitable business. This first period of overseas trading in hides was short-lived, however, because of the outbreak of war in this country in 1861.

Toward the end of the war, as food and leather become scarce in the South, the alligator again became a target. Hides were used for leather, and oil from alligators was used to lubricate machinery for the cotton industry. Meat from the tail and jowls, which tastes somewhat like fish, was used as food. Demand for hides lulled for a few years after the war, but about 1870 several United States tanneries began to process alligator hides. As far as large, natural populations of alligators were concerned, this was the beginning of the end. There is no way to determine exactly how many alligators were killed, but tannery records indicate at least **ten million** alligator hides were processed from 1870 until 1965. The true number is undoubtedly higher.

The heyday of alligator slaughter took place in the 1880s when populations were still fairly large. Approximately one quarter of all hides processed, more than 2.5 million skins, passed through tanneries from 1881 to 1891. As populations dwindled and alligator hides became harder to obtain, the prices skyrocketed. By the 1960s when laws were finally initiated to protect the alligator, populations were dangerously small.

Hide hunters around the turn of the century brought in thrity to forty skins per night. By the 1930s and 40s ten to twelve skins per night was a more common haul. By the 1950s a good night's work netted two or three skins. With hides becoming scarce, hide hunting increased in profitability.

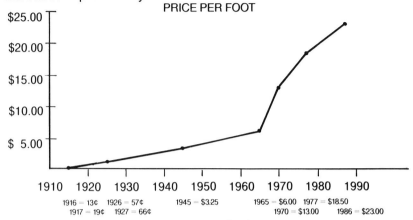

PRICE PER FOOT

1916 = 13¢	1926 = 57¢	1945 = $3.25
1917 = 19¢	1927 = 66¢	

1965 = $6.00	1977 = $18.50
1970 = $13.00	1986 = $23.00

Average values of alligator hides (price per foot).

Hide hunters were colorful characters. Tales of their cunning – and their lawlessness – have become legendary in gator country. Historically, gator hunting took place at night. Hunters outfitted themselves with a small skiff, headlamp, rifle, and knife. They poled or motored through the water until they spotted the red reflections of alligator eyes. Lone "floaters" were shot before they submerged. Gators were pulled from their dens by noosing them or poking them until they bit down on a long, hooked pole. Once extracted, they were shot or chopped behind the head with a machete. In Louisiana, hunters baited large hooks with chicken or blackbirds and suspended them just above the water. Gators strangled after taking the bait.

Once an alligator was killed, a skilled hunter could skin it in a matter of minutes. Because of the bony plates in the neck and back, only the belly, throat, and under-tail skin of an alligator was taken. Hunters used a machete or sharp knife to cut the skin behind the head and along both sides, parallel to the backbone. Then it was carefully cut away under the throat and belly, salted, and rolled for storage or shipping. The rest of the carcass, about 95 percent of the body, was usually left to rot.

By 1960 it was evident that overhunting and the loss of swamp habitat were taking a great toll on alligator pouplations. Large numbers of baby alligators were being sold to tourists or shipped to pet stores in the North. Many of these died from pneumonia or calcium deficiencies. During the early 1960s about the only places alligators could be found in the wild were a few wildlife refuges and parks.

A poacher in Everglades National Park was caught red-handed in the late 1960s. His skiff and slain gators were held as evidence. NPS Photo.

The Poacher's Era

In response to declining alligator populations, several southern states began to shorten or close seasons on alligator hunting. In 1944 Florida closed hunting for all alligators during the breeding season and protected gators under four feet year-round. All gator hunting was illegal in the state after 1961. In Louisiana a 1962 law prohibited taking alligators under two feet and by 1966 the season was completely closed. Closing seasons made hides harder to obtain, but demand for alligator leather items was at an all-time high. In the late 1960s alligator shoes cost $70 to $350 per pair, handbags brought $150 to $250, and luggage sold for up to $1,000 per piece. Raw hides sold for about $6.00 per foot and up, which meant that professional alligator hunters could make $10,000 to $12,000 a year. When seasons were shortened or closed, some hunters poached alligators in the off-season or in protected areas and shipped them for sale in states that still had open seasons.

After Florida outlawed alligator hunting in 1961, poaching continued to be a million-dollar business. Poachers hunted from cars along canals, from skiffs, and from "fishing" boats, often in protected park and refuge waters. They cached their hides or, if approached in the field, kicked their guns and hides overboard just before the conservation officer arrived. A favorite trick was to toss out some trash nearby, which would float there until they could return to pick up guns and hides later. To the frustration of park rangers and conservation officers, many piles of skinned carcasses and alligator bones were found in the mid-1960s, but poachers were seldom caught. One man supposedly cached his hides along the Tamiami Trail, U.S. Highway 41, which runs through the Everglades. When all was clear, he would radio to his partner in a small plane to land on the highway at dawn, pick up the hides, and fly them to another state to be sold.

Florida hides were smuggled into Georgia and Louisiana, which had open seasons until the mid-1960s, and sold to processors from Chicago and New York. Even if poachers were caught red-handed, which seldom happened in spite of diligent enforcement efforts by state and federal agents, penalties were a maximum fine of $1,000 or a year in jail. Local judges rarely imposed maximum sentences, so the few offenders caught usually ended up paying minor fines. Most fines could be, and usually were, recovered in several nights' work.

It was estimated in 1968 that 97 percent of all alligator goods came from illegal sources. In 1969 the **Miami Herald** estimated 250 poachers were making a full-time living from alligators hunted illegally in Everglades National Park and surrounding South Florida marshes. Another two to three thousand were believed to be occasional poachers. The newspaper quoted South Florida conservation officers, who speculated twenty to fifty thousand alligators were illegally slaughtered each year. It became evident that closing hunting seasons was not the solution to saving the American alligator. Even though "protected" by hunting laws in 95 percent of its range, the alligator was added to the list of endangered species in 1967.

Traffic in alligator hides did not begin to taper off, however, until laws were passed to stop the tanners and marketers. In 1969 the State of New York passed the Mason-Smith Act, which banned the sale of endangered species and their products within the state. Later Pennsylvania, Massachusetts, Connecticut, and California passed similar laws. In addition, the Lacey Act was amended by Congress to prohibit interstate trade in reptile hides obtained illegally. Unfortunately this did not entirely stop the slaughter of crocodilians. When domestic sources of alligator and crocodile hides were outlawed, dealers turned to caiman and crocodile hides exported from Central and South America, Africa, and Southeast Asia. Most of these species are now endangered. The Lacey Act also made importing poached hides or those exported from illegal sources unlawful. Yet, in the late 1960s and early 70s American tanners were importing about 75,000 hides per year. In 1973 the Convention on International

Trade in Endangered Species (CITES), a multi-national organization, outlawed the trade in endangered plants and animals among member nations. In the same year, Congress enacted the Federal Endangered Species Act. Since then, a number of individuals and corporations have been prosecuted, and the trade in illegal crocodilian hides has diminished.

Alligators Today

Three categories are used to describe alligator populations. "Endangered" refers to numbers so low gators may become extinct. "Threatened" indicates an increasing population. "Threatened due to similarity of appearance" means alligators have recovered, but trade in gator skins and products must be monitored because of their close resemblance to other endangered crocodilians.

Once alligator poaching was controlled, gator populations rebounded quickly. Unlike many endangered species, adequate numbers of adult alligators remained in the breeding population. Their offspring flourished in protected wetlands. A decade after serious protection began, gator populations in many areas were approaching turn-of-the-century levels.

Louisiana led the way in removing gators from the endangered list. By the late 1970s, populations in three Louisiana parishes increased enough to be considered recovered. At that time, alligators in the rest of Louisiana, plus Florida, Texas, and parts of Georgia and South Carolina were designated as threatened. A few years later, these populations were also upgraded to recovered status. In 1987, the U.S. Fish & Wildlife Service changed all of the remaining populations to the threatened due to similarity of appearance category. This means alligators are now recovered and approaching carrying capacity levels in their remaining habitat.

Louisiana tested a short open hunting season in one parish in 1972. Alligator populations increased enough that by 1981 hunting was permitted, under close supervision, in the entire state. Texas has allowed the limited hunting of alligators since 1984. In Florida, an experimental alligator harvest was begun on three lakes near Gainesville in 1981. It was expanded to six additional lakes throughout the state in the mid-1980s, and by late in this decade, a state-wide hunting program is expected.

In most areas where hunting is allowed, gators may be taken only during daylight hours. Killing alligators smaller than four feet is prohibited. Tags are attached to the skins after the animals are harvested, and the tag numbers are tracked until the hide enters the tannery. This strict regulation of the sale of hides has prevented new outbreaks of poaching. Reasonable hunting quotas have allowed gator populations to continue to increase.

Alligator leather remains popular for boots, wallets, and handbags. Hides have been purchased by American, French, Italian, and Japanese tanners for as much as $23 per foot. Alligator meat is gaining popularity. It retails at $4 to $7 per pound. About half is purchased for private consumption, and the remainder is sold at restaurants and fish markets. Gator teeth are sold locally for jewelry, and skulls are marketed to biological supply houses.

"Nuisance" alligators, animals that have grown too bold around people, pose a problem for state game officials. If the animals can easily be removed to prevent further interaction with humans, they are relocated. When the animals are too large to be moved or so conditioned to begging that they will return to civilization, they are shot. States with large alligator populations work with private trappers who assist in capturing, or if necessary, killing, nuisance gators. The trappers share with state wildlife agencies the proceeds from the sale of hides and other parts of these nuisance gators.

Alligator farming is commercially important in Florida and Louisiana. Some alligator farms are in business to sell hides and meat. Others market live animals to zoos, animal dealers, and research labs. Many also welcome tourists.

At gator farms, adult alligators are usually held in large fenced pens with one or more ponds in them. The large gators are fed fish, chicken, or red meat. They eat once a week. After the females nest each spring, eggs are collected and incubated in special chambers. Young alligators are raised in holding pens, where they are fed ground fish and red meat two or three times a week.

In order to prevent illegal alligator products from entering the market, alligator farmers are required to obtain permits for the sale of skins, meat, and other alligator parts. Hides are tagged in the same manner as those obtained during hunting seasons and must be accompanied by export permits when moved across state lines.

VII – Searching For Answers

Alligators were regarded merely as curiosities until early in this century. Little scientific research was done on their life histories. One of the first to study and write about the alligator was E.A. McIlhenny. McIlhenny's research centered on gators near his home in southern Louisiana and culminated with the publication of **An Alligator's Life History** in 1935.

At Everglades National Park, concerns about alligators surfaced in the late 1950s. Ranger Richard Stokes began reporting his observations of alligators made while on backcountry patrols. Poaching and water diversion outside the park were reducing both the number of alligators and the habitat available to them. Stokes experimented with dynamiting holes in the bedrock to try to reach the lowered water table. His success was questionable as far as the gators were concerned, but it did bring national attention to their plight.

Dr. Frank Craighead, Sr., a park biologist, documented the decline of alligator populations in southern Florida. He also studied the ecological role of alligator holes as they related to birds, turtles, fishes, and other marsh inhabitants. About the same time, the Florida Game and Fresh Water Fish Commission conducted gator research in the water conservation areas north of the park. Tommy Hines, Michael Fogarty, and Carlton Chappel studied growth rates, sex ratios, and movements of alligators. They noosed about 1,000 gators, measured them, and marked them with numbered tags. Later recaptures of some of the same individuals provided information on growth and movement.

Also during the 1960s, Robert Chabreck studied alligators on the Rockefeller Wildlife Refuge in Louisiana. He tagged over 2,000 animals in six years. His research focused on the movements of alligators as they related to age, sex, and fluctuations in water levels. He also studied the growth rates of and habitat types used by Louisiana alligator populations.

Louisiana biologists Ted Joanen and Larry McNease have continued to collect data on the alligators at Rockefeller Refuge for nearly two decades. Among their projects have been radio telemetry studies of seasonal alligator movements and research on alligator nesting, incubation temperatures, growth rates, and nutrition. They have also experimented with various techniques of alligator farming.

In the mid-1970s biologist Jim Kushlan began to study how the alligators in Shark Slough, the main watershed at Everglades National Park, related to populations of wading birds and freshwater fishes.

Venturing into the marsh by airboat at night, Kushlan and his assistants captured alligators in a 3.9-square-mile study plot. The animals were weighed, measured, sexed, and tagged. When recaptured, they were again weighed and measured, and any movements from the site of their first capture were noted.

Researchers recording length measurements.

Several of the larger alligators were fitted with neck collars that carried radio transmitters. Their signals were monitored using telemetry equipment in the airboat, park aircraft, and at fixed bases. These studies and similar research in Louisiana have been useful in determining the territorial sizes of adult male and female alligators and in discovering patterns of seasonal movement.

Sampling the food alligators eat has been revealing. The stomach contents of small gators that had been poached in Florida some years ago were analyzed by game officers. These alligators had been eating mostly snails and crayfish. In the late 1970s stomach contents of live alligators in the Everglades were collected. Food samples included small fish, water insects, snails, and birds.

Alligator behavior is beginning to be understood more clearly thanks to other researchers. Kent Vliet observed captive gators at an alligator farm in northern Florida and wild gators at Okefenokee for a number of years. He concentrated on courting and mating behaviors and believes that alligators communicate visually, as well as by bellowing.

A few large alligators were fitted with radio transmitter collars and tracked as they moved about in the Everglades National Park study area. Photo – Pat Toops.

R. Howard Hunt has focused on maternal behavior of female alligators at Okefenokee. He confirmed that some female alligators do excavate their nests at the time of hatching and carry the young in their mouths to the water. He documented the successful nesting of a blind female alligator, indicating that the senses of smell and hearing are of great importance to an alligator's survival. Hunt also studied predation on alligator nests at Okefenokee, finding that black bears and raccoons are responsible for most nest destruction.

Dr. Kushlan linked nesting failures in the Everglades to untimely releases of water during the nesting season. Unnatural flooding has been avoided by a new management plan that meters releases of water into the park based on natural rainfall patterns. Studies that analyze the relationship between surface water levels and the successful reproduction of various wildlife communities continue to be a priority in Everglades National Park.

Some may think it cruel to capture and tag alligators. Recaptured animals, however, show no adverse effects from wearing their tags or collars. Casualties have been kept to a minimum. Researchers frequently blindfold the animals while gathering data so a gator's association with humans will be minimized. The knowledge gained from these studies has helped alligator populations recover. Some of the information is now being applied to American crocodiles and other endangered crocodilians. Thus, techniques pioneered in studying alligators may lead to the survival of endangered species worldwide.

This nine-foot alligator, captured in Shark Slough, was among the largest studied in Everglades National Park. Photo – Mark Salzburg.

VIII – The Web of Life

Alligators often sun atop rocks or on mud banks near the water. Their well-being and that of the Southeastern wetlands depends upon our willingness to conserve natural areas.

Where Do We Stand?

Members of the American Alligator Council tried to estimate the number of gators remaining in the U.S. in 1970. They concluded that about a million animals resided in the southeast. Although a million alligators may seem to be a substantial number, during the heyday of alligator hunting in the late 1880s, a million alligators were killed in only three or four years.

Several methods are presently used to estimate alligator populations. Aerial surveys of nests and night counts of animals seen along canals, rivers, and ponds are two of the most popular techniques. Neither of these methods accounts for all of the alligators in the population, so over the years, "multiplier factors" have been tested. They adjust raw data from counts to more accurate estimates of total alligator populations. Although such estimates are beneficial in showing increases or decreases from year to year, it should be remembered they represent best guesses rather than an individual tally of each animal present.

Biologists using this "best guess" method of estimating populations believe there are over 100,000 alligators in Texas. Most are found along the Gulf Coast northward from Corpus Christi. In the mid-1980s Louisiana biologists concluded the state's alligators had increased to turn-of-the-century levels. Louisiana alligators are most numerous in coastal marshes, where their populations are still increasing at about 10% per year. Approximately 500,000 alligators presently reside in that state.

Mississippi and Alabama's alligators are also concentrated in the coastal counties. A few gators inhabit rivers and streams that meander north from the coasts or reside in inland lakes and ponds. The alligator population in these two states totals around 6,000.

Okefenokee National Wildlife Refuge is one of the most likely places in Georgia to see alligators. Managers at Okefenokee believe the refuge hosts between 10,000 and 12,000 gators. Statewide, the population is about ten times that figure. In addition to coastal marshes, Georgia's alligators inhabit farm ponds, lakes, and rice impoundments in southern and eastern regions of the state.

South Carolina is home to approximately 60,000 gators. Biologists feel the population is stable. Alligators reach the northern limit of their range in North Carolina. Most of the state's approximately 2,000 alligators are found along the coast southward from Albemarle Sound.

Florida hosts the largest alligator population of any state. Biologists estimate one million gators reside there. That figure seems large, but several decades ago Dr. Frank Craighead surveyed Everglades alligator holes. He postulated that before the settlement of South Florida, there were as many as one million alligators living in the area south of the Tamiami Trail. This is the area presently occupied by Everglades National Park and part of Big Cypress National Preserve.

Just two decades ago alligator populations were at an all-time low. Biologists are encouraged that in the past few years alligators have nearly doubled in number. At this writing, there are believed to be at least 1.75 million alligators in the southeastern U.S. Under adequate protection, animals once faced with extinction have recovered. The rapid increase in alligator populations will not continue, however. Game officials in most states report that alligators multiplied quickly through the mid-1970s, but have been reproducing at a much slower rate since then. Apparently these animals have neared the capacity of the remaining wetlands to provide food and cover.

The greatest threat to alligators now is loss of habitat. Countless wetlands have been drained, filled, and converted to farmlands or residential areas. There simply are not as many lakes, ponds, and marshes as in pre-settlement days. Thus preserves such as the Everglades, Big Cypress, and Okefenokee are increasingly important as population centers for American alligators.

The Prognosis

Alligator populations are considered healthy as long as the number of individuals that die each year does not exceed the number of young that hatch and survive. Throughout their range, alligators have reproduced to fill much of the habitat that will support them. This is an encouraging accomplishment. But in comparing present population levels to those of a little over a century ago, alligators are still nowhere as abundant as they once were.

The difference results from the millions of acres of wetland habitat that have been removed from the natural system. Drainage of these marshes has disrupted nesting and feeding areas of countless birds, mammals, and fishes in addition to gators. Just as alligator numbers have been drastically reduced, so have the populations of many other species of wetlands plants and animals. All are part of a delicately balanced ecosystem. In nature, no one species is more or less important than any other.

There is no easy solution to this problem. We cannot reverse development that has already taken place. It should, however, make us more aware of habitat losses occurring worldwide – from oil development in the arctic tundra to destruction of tropical rainforests.

The alligator is but one strand in a delicate web of life that reaches out to involve us all. In the past we have broken many strands. The timber wolf, the grizzly bear, and the panther are other large predators which, like the alligator, influence the health of our environment. Before too many strands are broken, before the damage is irreparable, we need to learn to fit ourselves back into the natural system with as little disturbance as possible. We are managing to find room for people and the American alligator, too. We should use this success story as a model for preserving other endangered species.

Worldwide, we must conserve areas for the study and protection of remaining crocodilians and the countless other plants and animals that share their habitats. We should remove our biases through education. Alligators and their kin are not slimy, vicious man-killers. They are unique and highly complex survivors of a long-ago world. They are also indicators of the quality of life on this planet. By learning more about them, we will ultimately know more about ourselves and our environment.

Bibliography

Blair, Jonathan. "A Bad Time to be a Crocodile," *National Geographic,* 153 (1): 90-114 (January 1978).

Campbell, George R. *Jaws, Two: The Story of Sanibel's Alligators and Other Crocodilians.* Sanibel, FL: Sanibel-Captiva Conservation Foundation, 1981.

Chabreck, Robert H. *The American Alligator – Past, Present, and Future.* Grand Chenier, LA: Louisiana Wildlife and Fisheries Commission, 1967.

Chabreck, Robert H. and Ted Joanen. "Growth Rates of American Alligators in Louisiana," *Herpetologica* 35(1): 51-57 (March 1979).

————. *Methods of Determining the Size and Composition of Alligator Populations in Louisiana.* Grand Chenier, LA: Louisiana Wildlife and Fisheries Commission, 1966.

Chiasson, Robert B. *Laboratory Anatomy of the Alligator.* Dubuque, IA: W.C. Brown, 1962.

Craighead, Frank C. "The Role of the Alligator in Shaping Plant Communities and Maintaining Wildlife in the Southern Everglades," *Florida Naturalist,* 41 (1&2): (January & April 1968).

Coulson, Roland A. and Thomas Hernanden. *Biochemistry of the Alligator.* Baton Rouge: Louisiana State University Press, 1964.

Ferguson, Mark W.J. and Ted Joanen. "Temperature of Egg Incubation Determines Sex in Alligator mississippiensis," *Nature,* 296 (5860): 850-853 (April 1982).

Fogarty, Michael J. and Jean David Albury. *Late Summer Food Habits of Small Alligators from L-38 Canal, Everglades Wildlife Management Area.* Ft. Lauderdale: Florida Game and Fresh Water Fish Commission, 1966.

Hunt, R. Howard. "Nest Excavation and Neonate Transport in Wild *Alligator mississippiensis," Journal of Herpetology,* 1987.

————. "Predation of Alligator Nests in Okefenokee Swamp National Wildlife Refuge, Georgia," *Proceedings of 8th Crocodile Specialist Group, Species Survival Commission, International Union for Conservation of Nature and Natural Resources,* Quito, Ecuador, October 1986.

Jacobsen, Terri and James A. Kushlan. "Alligator Nest Flooding in the Southern Everglades," *Proceedings of 7th Working Meeting of the Crocodile Specialist Group I.U.C.N.,* Caracas, Venezuela, October 1984.

Joanen, Ted. "Nesting Ecology of Alligators in Louisiana," *Proceedings of 23rd Annual Conference of the Southeastern Association of Game and Fish Commissioners,* 1969.

Joanen, Ted and Larry McNease. "Louisiana's Alligator Management Program," *Proceedings of Conference on Crocodile Conservation and Management,* Darwin, Australia, January 1985.

_____. "Nesting Chronology of the American Alligator and Factors Affecting Nesting in Louisiana," *Proceedings of the First Annual Alligator Production Conference,* Gainesville: University of Florida, February 1981.

_____. "Notes of the Reproductive Biology and Captive Propagation of the American Alligator," *Proceedings of the 29th Annual Conference of the Southeastern Assocation of Game and Fish Commissioners,* 1975.

_____. "A Telemetric Study of Adult Male Alligators on Rockefeller Refuge, Louisiana," *Proceedings of the 26th Annual Conference of Game and Fish Commissioners,* 1972.

Joanen, Ted, et al. "The Effects of Incubation Temperature on American Alligator Hatchling Size and Growth Rate," *Proceedings of Conference on Crocodile Conservation and Management,* Darwin, Australia, January 1985.

King F. Wayne. "The American Alligator," *National Parks and Conservation Magazine,* May 1972, p. 15-18.

Kushlan, James A. *An Ecological Study of an Alligator Pond in the Big Cypress Swamp of Southern Florida.* Coral Gables: University of Miami, 1972.

_____. "Observations on Maternal Behavior in the American Alligator, *Alligator mississippiensis,"* *Herpetologica* 29 (3): 256-257 (September 1973).

_____. "Observations on the Role of the American Alligator in the South Florida Wetlands," *Copeia* 4:993-996 (December 1971).

Lang, Jeffery W. "Amphibious Behavior of *Alligator mississippiensis:* Roles of a Circadian Rhythm and Light," *Science* 101:3 (February 1976).

McIlhenny, Edward A. *The Alligator's Life History.* Boston: Christopher Publishing House, 1935.

Neill, Wilfred T. *The Last of the Ruling Reptiles: Alligators, Crocodiles, and Their Kin.* New York: Columbia Press, 1971.

Stokes, Richard A. *Report on the American Alligator.* Homestead, FL: Everglades National Park (unpublished), 1966

Thompson, Bruce C., Floyd E. Potter, Jr., and William C. Brownlee. *Management Plan for the American Alligator in Texas.* Austin: Texas Parks and Wildlife Department, 1984.

The Author

Connie Toops spent six years as a seasonal naturalist at Everglades National Park. During that time she observed alligators feeding, fighting, courting, and raising their young in the Everglades marshes.

In 1978 Connie began a career as a nature photographer and writer. One of her first projects was a book about alligators – a book designed to answer typical questions asked by visitors to southeastern parks and wildlife refuges. Since then she has also written *Birds of South Florida, The Story Behind the Scenery: National Seashores, Crater Lake National Park Trails,* and a chapter in the *Reader's Digest* book, "Our National Parks." Her articles and photos appear in numerous national conservation magazines.

The Publisher

This book is published by Florida National Parks & Monuments Association, Inc., a non-profit organization. Proceeds from sales make publications like this one possible and assist in supporting the educational, scientific, historical, and visitor services programs of Everglades National Park, Biscayne National Park, Fort Jefferson National Monument, Big Cypress National Preserve, and other activities within the National Park Service.

For more information on Association activities contact: Florida National Parks & Monuments Association, Inc., P.O. Box 279, Homestead, FL 33030.